Handmade
Embroidered
Greetings Cards

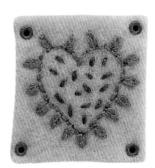

For my daughter Barley

Handmade
Embroidered
Greetings Cards

Dorothy Wood

SEARCH PRESS

First published in Great Britain 2004

Search Press Limited
Wellwood, North Farm Road,
Tunbridge Wells, Kent TN2 3DR

Text copyright © Dorothy Wood 2004

Photographs by Charlotte de la Bédoyère,
Search Press Studios except those on pages 1–8, 10, 15,
16/17, 21 (bottom), 22/23, 28, 29, 33 (bottom), 34/35,
40/41, 45 (bottom), 46/47 and 48 which are by
Roddy Paine Photographic Studios

Photographs and design copyright © Search Press Ltd. 2004

ISBN 1 903975 79 4

The Publishers and author can accept no responsibility for
any consequences arising from the information, advice or
instructions given in this publication.

Suppliers
If you have difficulty in obtaining any of the materials and
equipment mentioned in this book, then please visit the
Search Press website for details of suppliers:
www.searchpress.com

Alternatively, you can write to the Publishers at the address
above, for a current list of stockists, including firms who
operate a mail-order service.

Publishers' note
All the step-by-step photographs in this book feature the
author, Dorothy Wood, demonstrating how to make
embroidered greetings cards. No models have been used.

*I would like to thank the following companies for
providing materials for the book: the
scrapbookhouse for card, eyelets, snaps, vellum,
decorative paperclips, hole punch and setting
tools; Debbie Cripps and Mill Hill for decorative
buttons; James Hare Silks for silk dupion and
organza; Craft Creations and Card Art for cards
and paper; Impress Cards for polypropylene bags
and cards; Macleod Craft Marketing for the
Caron variegated pima cotton; and Ribbon
Designs for the embroidery ribbon.*

*Special thanks go to Roz Dace for commissioning
the book, to my editor, John Dalton and to
Charlotte de la Bédoyère and Roddy Paine for the
excellent photography.*

Printed in Spain by A. G. Elkar S. Coop. 48180 Loiu (Bizkaia)

Contents

Introduction

For me, one of the nicest things to happen on a birthday, anniversary or other special occasion is to receive a card and, although there are lots of lovely cards in the shops, it is always that bit more special if the card is handmade too.

I love making cards myself and, because I am also mad about embroidery and textiles, like to use fabrics and stitches to make pretty, tactile designs. Although I prefer very contemporary, simple designs, it is essential to match the card to the person, so I have created a range of cards using a variety of embroidery techniques and styles that would be suitable to send to family, friends and colleagues.

The designs are divided into six projects, each concentrating on a different style. From simple stitching on paper to using appliqué or decorative buttons, there are lots or ideas that add a different dimension to the stitching. Traditional embroiderers can enjoy the fun animals worked in long and short stitch or for a complete change, stitch the pretty floral designs in ribbon embroidery. The first card uses only straight stitches and then two or three new stitches are introduced in each section. You can stitch the cards in any order, but if you are new to embroidery use the book as an embroidery workshop, building on your skills and learning new techniques in easy stages.

To give the cards a contemporary feel, I have drawn on the plethora of paper crafting techniques using translucent paper, eyelets and decorative paperclips and buttons to complement the embroidery designs.

I hope you enjoy making the cards as much as I have and are inspired to create some designs of your own.

Happy stitching.

Materials

Fabrics

Embroidery fabrics   Any fabric that can easily be fitted in an embroidery hoop without marking will be suitable for embroidery. For cards, finer fabrics are ideal as they are not too bulky. A lightweight soft suiting fabric with a plain weave such as Panama fabric is ideal for embroidery. Add a top layer of silk organza to give a subtle touch of colour. Silk dupion, which is available in a range of gorgeous colours is also ideal, giving a luxury finish to a celebration card.

Backing fabric   Fine cotton lawn or poplin is an ideal backing fabric. A backing fabric allows you to begin and finish off threads invisibly on the reverse side. It also enables you to use a fine fabric such as organza or silk dupion for embroidery.

Felt   This is available in a range of colours and is ideal for making simple cards as it can be trimmed with straight or fancy scissors without fraying. Felt is thick enough to be used without backing fabric and can be attached to the front of a card using eyelets, snaps or double-sided sticky tape.

Interfacing   Iron-on interfacing can be used in place of backing fabric when embroidering designs. It allows the fabric to be trimmed to shape with a minimum of fraying. Choose a weight to suit the fabric.

Wadding   Use this to pad the embroidered fabric when it is fitted in an aperture card. Use a low-loft wadding (sold for making quilts) so that the padding is not too bulky. Cut it to the size and shape of the aperture.

Bonding web   This is a mesh layer that allows two layers of fabric to be bonded together using an iron. It is used in appliqué and prevents the fabric fraying.

Cards and paper

Card blanks   The range of aperture and single-fold card blanks is vast. Single-fold cards are suitable for designs worked on felt or those tucked in a polypropylene bag. Aperture cards in a range of shapes, colours and sizes are ideal for mounting the more traditional embroideries.

Card   There is a huge range of card available in an almost infinite variety of colours. Look out for unusual card such as duo card (coloured differently on each side) as well as metallic and textured finishes.

Translucent paper   Parchment paper and vellum are just two of the names used for translucent paper. Translucent paper is available in a range of colours and patterns. Tracing paper is a lighter weight paper that can be used to transfer designs for embroidery. There are also single-fold card blanks available in a heavyweight vellum.

Baking parchment   This paper is really for lining baking tins but it is also ideal for preventing the iron sticking to bonding web.

Threads and ribbons

Embroidery thread   The most popular is six-stranded embroidery cotton. For best results, separate all six strands first and then thread the required number in the needle. For stitching on felt use a thicker thread such as coton perlé or three-ply pima cotton, and try variegated threads for unusual effects.

Metallic thread   Any metallic thread that can be passed through the eye of a needle and pulled through fabric without fraying is suitable for embroidery. Metallic machine embroidery thread is particularly suitable and this is available in a wide range of colours.

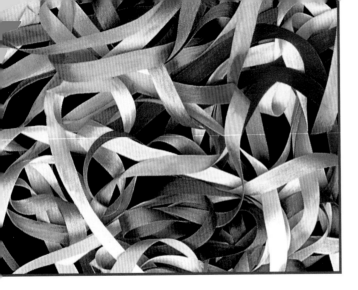

Embroidery ribbon   Ribbon for embroidery differs from ordinary ribbon in that it does not have a woven selvedge. It is easier to stitch and has a lovely soft appearance. Silk is the best fibre for embroidery. Choose from a plain silk or sheer organza for different effects.

Embellishments

Snaps and eyelets   These are an easy way to attach an embroidery design to a card blank. The snaps and eyelets are fitted using special tools (see tools) and come in a range of colours and sizes.

Beads and sequins   Use seed beads and sequins to embellish embroidered cards. Avoid beads that are too large as they may get damaged in the post.

Decorative buttons   Some buttons are specially designed for embroidery. Use the different styles to inspire your own embroidery designs. Cover with a layer of bubble wrap if sending in the post.

Decorative paper clips   Use decorative paper clips or tiny clothes pegs to attach embroidered designs to the card blank. You could shape your own with fine wire.

Polypropylene bags   These clear bags are ideal for protecting embroidered designs and allow them to be mounted on a single-fold card. They are available in a range of sizes.

Tools

Embroidery hoop   Use a wooden hoop close in size to the design you are stitching. For better grip, bind the inner hoop with narrow white cotton tape.

Scissors   Keep a selection of scissors for different tasks: strong ones to cut paper and card; small embroidery scissors to snip threads; and pinking shears to trim felt so that it has an attractive zigzag edge.

Needles and pins   Crewel (or embroidery) needles have large eyes to take embroidery thread – I used a No. 9 for all the projects in this book. For ribbon embroidery, use a No. 18 chenille needle which has a longer eye. Use dressmaker's pins to mark the outline of an aperture before cutting and to prick holes in card prior to stitching.

Embroidery marker   Water-soluble markers are suitable for most embroidered cards as the design remains in place until the embroidery is complete. The marks are removed by spraying lightly with water.

Mouse mat   This is used for pricking designs when stitching on paper. If you do not have a computer, you could use a sheet of brightly coloured funky foam sold in most craft shops.

Hole punch, setting tool, hammer and mat   It is worth investing in this set of equipment if you use lots of eyelets and snaps. The hole punch and setting tools have interchangeable heads for different sized eyelets and snaps.

Craft knife, ruler and cutting mat   Always use a sharp blade in your craft knife and use a metal safety ruler to prevent accidents. Cut card on a self-healing cutting mat to prevent damage to work surfaces.

Gel pens   Gel pens have quick-drying, bright coloured ink that is ideal for craft work. Use metallic ink pens to create a border for stitched-paper, festive designs.

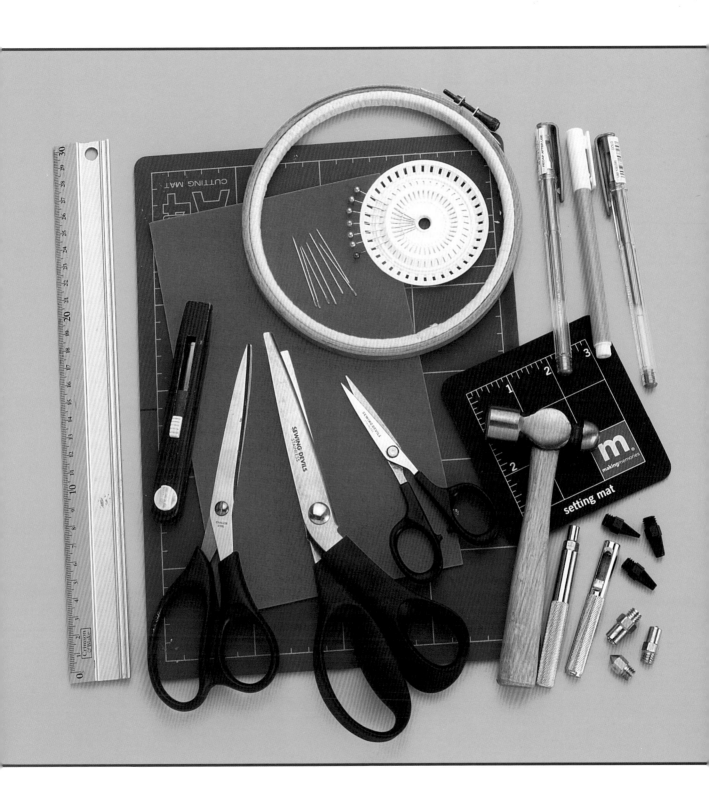

Festive star
Stitching on paper

Simple straight stitches can be used to create a variety of intricate thread patterns and motifs. In this elegant design, straight and back stitches are used to form a star shape which is then embellished with sequins. The combination of translucent parchment paper and metallic card is particularly effective for Christmas designs.

You will need

Silver card, 10cm (4in) square

Mouse (or foam) mat

Masking tape

Dressmaker's pin

Paper scissors

Embroidery scissors

Parchment paper, 10cm (4in) square

Silver gel pen

Double-sided sticky tape (DSST)

Silver metallic thread

No. 9 crewel needle

Star-shaped silver sequins

Single-fold, white hammer-finish card,
A6 (4 x 6in)

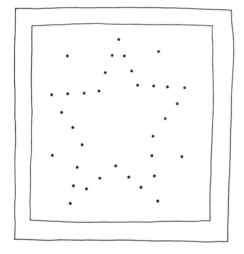

Full-size template

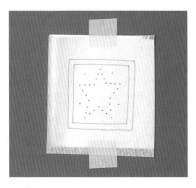

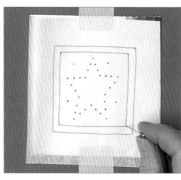

1. Place the piece of silver card on the mouse mat, then secure the template on top with masking tape.

2. Prick holes through each dot on the star, the four sequin holes and at each corner of the inner square.

3. Remove the template, then, using the holes as a guide, trim the piece of silver card to the size of the inner square.

4. Secure the parchment paper on top of the silver card, then use the silver gel pen to draw a square about 5mm (³/₁₆in) away from the edges of the silver card.

5. Prick holes through the parchment paper in the same places as the silver card.

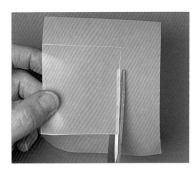

6. Trim along the outside edge of the silver line.

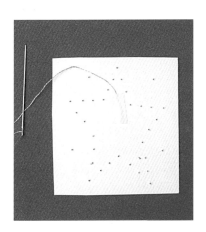

7. Thread a length of silver metallic thread on the needle, then use DSST to anchor the tail end on the back of the silver card adjacent to hole 1 (see thread stitching template).

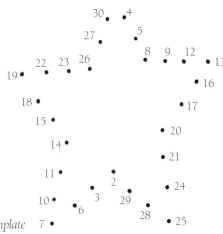

Thread stitching template

8. Place the parchment paper on top of the silver card and line up the holes. Bring the needle up through hole 1 on the template and down through hole 2.

9. Bring the needle up through hole 3 and down through hole 4.

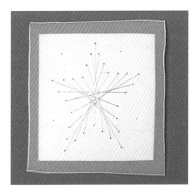

10. Carry on in this way taking the thread through consecutive holes until the design is complete. Anchor the thread on the back of the card with another piece of DSST and trim off the excess.

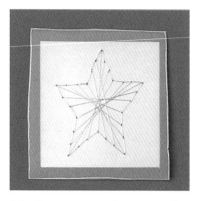

11. Anchor a second length of metallic thread, bring it out through hole 1, then take the needle down through hole 4 to start the back stitch outline of the star shape.

12. Bring the thread up through hole 5 and back down through hole 4.

13. Continue working round the edge of the star in this way to create a solid line of back stitch. Anchor the thread on the back of the silver card.

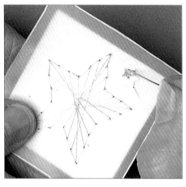

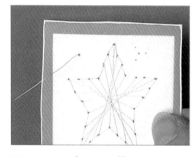

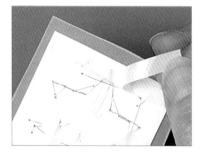

14. Secure another metallic thread on the back of the silver card and bring it up through one of the sequin holes. Pick up a sequin, let it drop down to the card, then stitch back through the paper and card at the bottom of the valley between two points of the star.

15. Bring the needle up through the centre of the sequin and down through the next-but-one valley. Repeat with a third stitch to secure the sequin. Attach the other sequins in the same way.

16. Stick three pieces of DSST on the back of the silver card and peel off the backing strips.

17. Carefully position the embroidered design on to the front of the white card to complete the project.

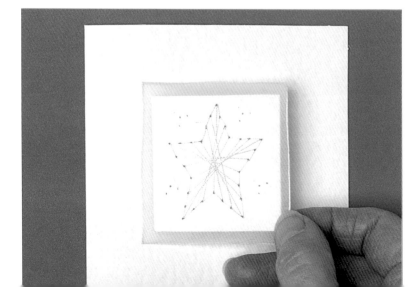

The finished card

Tip

Use bright colours of metallic thread, sequins and gel pens to make bold, colourful Christmas cards.

All of these Christmas motif cards were made in a similar manner to the card shown on pages 12–15, using a variety of metallic threads on different translucent and metallic papers.

To make your own stitched cards, draw out the design on paper, mark in the thread lines, then work out the order you need to stitch!

The Christmas tree and snowflake designs are quite easy to stitch, but you will get better, more accurate results if you draw templates on graph paper. Embellish the finished designs with white frosted seed beads, which can be stitched to the card or attached with tiny dots of glitter glue.

The winter tree design is stitched on 'white frost' parchment paper and flat translucent sequins are added as you stitch. Stitch the long branch lines first and then tuck the sequins under the thread before sewing in place with the shorter branch lines. The finished design is attached to the card using tiny 2mm ($^{1}/_{16}$in) eyelets.

The stitching sequence for the gold star card is slightly more complicated to work out, so I have included a thread stitching template (below).

To complement the cards, you could make some small gift tags using a simple stitch motif similar to the card design. Cut a piece of card to size and then mount the design on it.

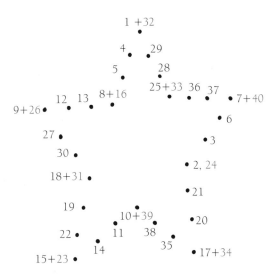

Thread stitching template for the gold star card. Start by bringing the thread out through hole 1, down through hole 2, up through hole 3, etc. The holes at the points of the star and those in the valleys between the points are used twice.

Be my Valentine
Stitching on felt

Felt is a super material to use for simple embroidered cards as it does not fray and can be cut to any shape or size. Felt is thick enough to be used without a backing fabric as the thread can be anchored invisibly on the back. This pretty design introduces chain stitch and lazy daisy stitch, and it is worked in an attractive variegated cotton. The three strands of cotton are separated and each worked as a single thread (which is similar in thickness to No. 8 coton perlé).

You will need
Purple felt, 10 x 12cm (4 x 5in)
Lightweight tracing paper
Pencil
Dressmaker's pins
Three-ply, pima cotton
(variegated sky blue and pink)
No. 9 crewel needle
Single-fold, lilac card, A6 (4 x 6in)
Embroidery scissors
Pinking shears
Masking tape
One pink and four lilac snaps
Hole punch, setting tool, setting mat and hammer

Tip
When using variegated cotton cut particular colour areas along the length to highlight features such as the centre flower in the heart design.

Full-size template

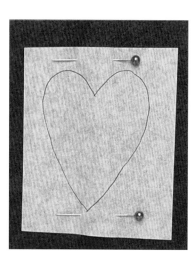

1. Trace the solid outline of the heart shape from the template on to lightweight tracing paper, then pin the traced motif in the middle of the piece of felt.

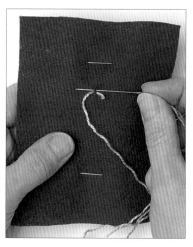

2. Separate a single strand of cotton, thread a length on a needle, then secure the tail end on the back of the felt with a tiny back stitch.

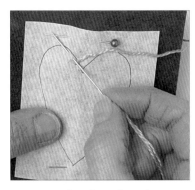

3. Bring the thread to the front, then, sewing through the paper and felt, work a row of running stitch just inside the marked line.

4. Carefully tear away the paper around the outside of the heart shape, then lift out the centre piece.

5. Bring the thread up at the valley of the heart shape and work a row of chain stitch. Make a small stitch from the start point, loop the thread under the needle . . .

6. . . . then pull the needle and thread through to close the loop.

7. Make the next small stitch from within the loop of the previous stitch. Repeat steps 6–7 round and down to the bottom of the heart.

8. When you reach the bottom point of the heart shape, anchor the last loop of the chain stitch by taking the thread down through the felt just outside the loop.

9. Work chain stitch up the other side of the heart shape, then work two rows of back stitch, one inside and one outside the existing stitching. Complete the border by working single chain stitches (also known as lazy daisy stitches) around the outer row of back stitch. Space the stitches evenly – say between pairs of back stitches.

10. Using a pink length of the thread, work five single chain stitches to form a flower in the centre of the heart motif. Leave a 3mm (¹/₈in) gap in the centre so that a snap can be inserted later on.

11. Fill the area around the flower with random running stitches – a technique which is known as seeding.

12. Use lengths of masking tape to mark the finished size of the felt, then use pinking shears to cut the felt to shape.

Tip
Take care to match the teeth of the pinking shears with the cut zigzag edge to ensure that the pattern is continuous.

13. Place the felt on the setting mat, then use the hole punch head of the setting tool and the hammer to make a hole in the centre of the flower.

14. Insert a pink snap in the hole, turn the felt over on to the setting mat, then use the other heads of the setting tool to set the snap.

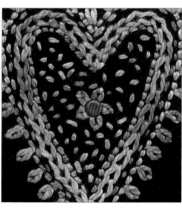

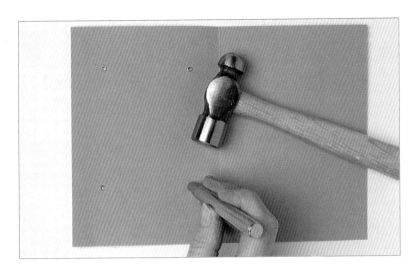

15. Open the card (face up) on the setting mat, position the embroidered felt on the right-hand side then punch a hole through all layers in each corner of the felt. Insert the snaps through the holes, carefully turn the card over, then set the snaps to complete the project.

The finished card

Tip

You could use the same stitches with different motifs to make a series of cards for a variety of occasions. Choose a variegated thread that tones with the felt and the card for best effect.

These pretty designs look quite different to the 'Be my Valentine' card but actually use all the same stitches. The contemporary look to the cards is achieved by using printed vellum paper available from scrapbook suppliers. As well as stripes, the paper is available in checks and polka dots in a range of colours. The small felt motifs, which are stitched on larger pieces of felt then pressed and trimmed to size, can be used to make a whole range of cards and gift tags.

To make the printed vellum stand out on the matching card colour, tear a square of white paper slightly smaller than the vellum paper. Attach the felt squares with simple stitches or eyelets, through both types of paper and then stick the finished design to the front of the card with double-sided sticky tape.

Matching gift tags are easy to make using just one of the little felt squares.

Plan your designs by drawing the squares and rectangles on paper and then use these as a cutting template.

Topiary tree
Stitching with buttons

Some decorative buttons are specially designed to use in embroidery and these can be very inspiring when designing cards. This topiary tree, for example, looks quite majestic in its large terracotta pot. Clusters of French knots form the oranges, stem stitch is used for the tree trunk and a variation of lazy daisy stitch, known as filled chain stitch, forms the leaves.

You will need
Cream Panama fabric
Cotton backing fabric
Low-loft wadding
Masking tape
Double-sided sticky tape (DSST)
Water-soluble marker and water sprayer
Two-fold, rectangular-aperture, orange card, A6 (4 x 6in)
Ruler
Embroidery hoop
No. 9 crewel needle
Six-stranded embroidery cotton (pale and dark tones of orange and green and brown)
Embroidery scissors
Terracotta pot button and four small buttons

Full-size template

1. Secure the fabric over the template, then use a water-soluble marker to trace the design.

2. Open the card, position the aperture centrally over the traced design and carefully mark its four corners on the fabric.

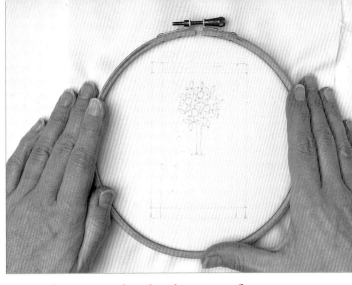

3. Draw a rectangle round the four points, then draw four lines approximately 6mm (¼in) in from the marks.

4. Lay the inner embroidery hoop on a flat surface, place the backing fabric and the marked fabric on top, then fit the outer hoop.

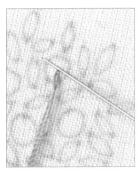

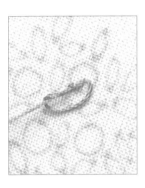

5. Work up the oranges with French knots. Using two strands of pale orange thread, bring the needle out in one of the marked circles. Take a tiny stitch next to where the thread emerged but leave the needle in the fabric.

6. Wrap the thread around the point of the needle two or three times . . .

7. . . . then pull the needle through.

8. When the knot is tight, take the needle back through the fabric close to the knot.

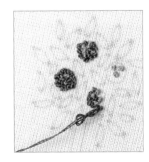

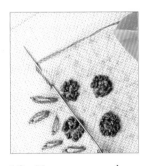

9. Work several pale orange French knots in each circle, then fill in the rest of the circles with dark orange French knots.

10. Use two strands of pale green cotton to work a single chain stitch for each leaf (see page 19).

11. Use three strands of dark green cotton to work a straight stitch down the centre of each leaf. The finished stitch is known as filled chain stitch.

 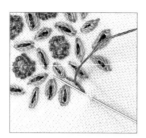 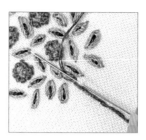 

12. Using one strand of two tones of brown, bring the needle out at the top of the trunk. Work a 6mm ($^1/_4$in) straight stitch bringing the needle back out 3mm ($^1/_8$in) away from where the thread first emerged.

13. Work another 6mm straight stitch and bring the needle out at the end of the first stitch. Continue down to the bottom of the trunk and sew in the thread end.

14. Use new thread to work a second row of stem stitch so that there is no fabric showing between.

15. Continue with more rows of stem stitch until the trunk is completely filled.

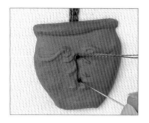 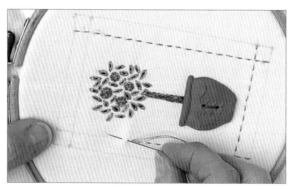 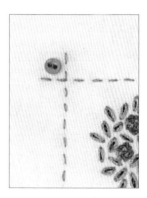

16. Use brown thread to sew on the button. Take the thread through the holes several times, then secure the thread on the reverse side with two tiny back stitches.

17. Work a row of running stitch along one of the marked lines around the topiary tree. Try to keep the stitches the same size and end a stitch at the cross point of the lines. Work along the other lines, keeping the stitches the same length and in the same position, especially where the lines cross.

18. Sew a small round button in each corner of the design.

19. Remove the fabric from the embroidery hoop, then spray it lightly with water to remove the marker pen lines. Press the fabric with an iron (set on warm) to remove any creases.

20. Cut the stitched fabric and backing fabric slightly over size.

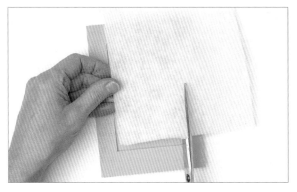

21. Cut a piece of low-loft wadding the same size as the aperture in the card.

22. Open up the card, lay it face down on the work surface and apply strips of DSST as shown. Remove the backing paper from the four strips round the aperture.

23. Lay the stitched fabric face up on the work surface and carefully position the card on top. Press down with your fingers to secure the DSST.

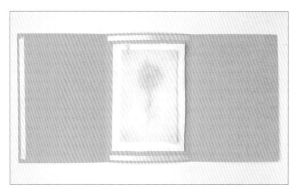

24. Turn the card over, place the wadding on the stitched fabric and remove the backing paper from the other strips of DSST.

25. Fold the front flap over so that it just catches on the strips of DSST at the top and bottom of the card.

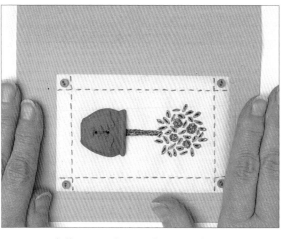

26. Carefully turn the card over, taking care not to disturb the wadding, then apply pressure to secure all the DSST.

Tip

When using large
buttons, you might find
it useful to use small glue
dots or silicone adhesive
to stick them to the
fabric before stitching
them in place.

Opposite

*Buttons for embroidery come in all shapes and sizes, and the embroidery
around the button can be as easy or complicated as you like. To make a
very simple card, choose a large heart button and use very basic stitches to
create the pretty design. You can use appliqué to change areas of the
background colour before stitching; the 'grass' in the birdhouse design, for
example, looks like fabric paint but is simply appliquéd organza.*

New baby
Stitching with appliqué

Appliqué is a simple way to add areas of colour or motifs on to the main fabric. The fabric is applied using bonding web, a fine mesh that fuses the two layers of fabric together when ironed. The design can then be embellished with simple embroidery stitches. Coral stitch is used for the curved lines and couching for the straight lines. Tête de boeuf, a variation of chain stitch, is used to decorate the body of the pram. The appliqué design is backed with iron-on interfacing (which helps prevent the fraying and adds body to the fabric) and is trimmed to fit inside a polypropylene bag. This alternative method of mounting a design can be used for other simple embroideries.

You will need
Fusible bonding web

Pencil

Silk dupion (pale pink, deep pink and white)

Pink organza

Six-stranded embroidery cotton
(pale and deep tones of both pink and blue)

No. 9 crewel needle

Iron

Embroidery scissors

Baking parchment or silicone paper

Embroidery hoop

Water-soluble marker and water sprayer

Iron-on interfacing

Decorative paper clip

Polypropylene bag, 7 x 12cm (2 $^3/_4$ x 4 $^3/_4$in)

Single-fold, pink-parchment card,
12 x 17cm (4 $^3/_4$ x 6 $^1/_2$in)

Craft knife

Tip
When working the wheels, aim to make twelve coral stitch knots around the rim so that you can make six spokes.

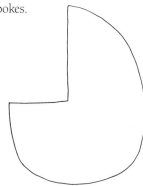

Full-size template for the embroidered design, and a reverse-image template for the body of the pram.

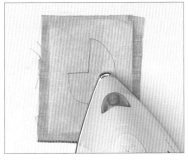

1. Trace the reverse image of the pram shape on to bonding web. Place the bonding web, paper side up, on the deep pink silk dupion and press with a medium hot iron.

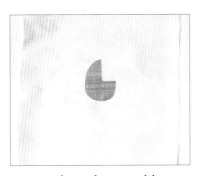

2. Cut along the pencil line and peel off the backing paper. Lay the appliqué shape (right side up) in the centre of the white silk dupion and press with a medium hot iron.

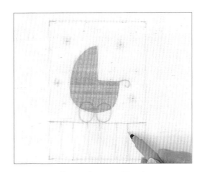

3. Lay the white silk dupion over the embroidery template, aligning the pram shape, then use the water-soluble marker to trace the design directly through the fabric.

4. Iron 5cm (2in) squares of bonding web on to the pale pink and deep pink dupion and the pink organza.

5. Cut the fabric into strips to match the depth of the pavement, then cut individual paving slabs.

6. Remove the backing paper and carefully place all the slabs in position with the bonding web side face down.

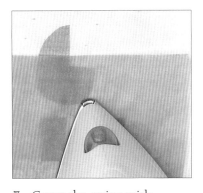

7. Cover the strips with baking parchment (to protect the iron) and press with a medium hot iron.

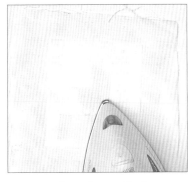

8. Turn the white silk dupion face down, then iron a piece of interfacing on the reverse of the white silk dupion. This will prevent the fabric fraying when trimmed to size.

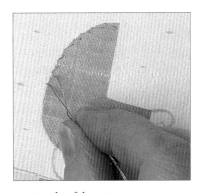

9. Fit the fabric in an embroidery hoop, then, using one strand of deep pink thread, catch the edge of the pram shape with a series of small, angled straight stitches.

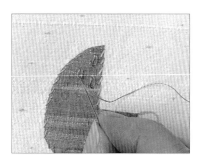

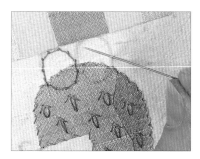

10. Referring to the template, work the tête de boeuf decoration. Use one strand of blue thread to make a series of single chain stitches . . .

11. . . . then work two small angular straight stitches beneath each chain stitch.

12. Start the coral stitch by bringing the thread out at the edge of the pram and making a tiny stitch 3mm ($\frac{1}{8}$in) along the rim of the wheel.

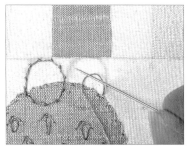

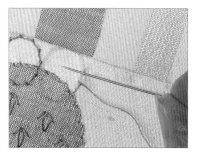

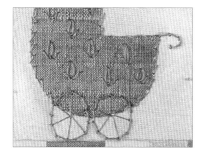

13. Wrap the thread around the needle . . .

14. . . . pull the thread through to form a knot, then start another stitch 3mm ($\frac{1}{8}$in) further round the rim.

15. Work round the wheels, then stitch the pram handle. Work straight stitch spokes from every second knot on the rim into the centre.

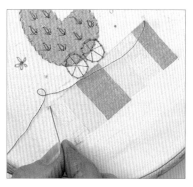

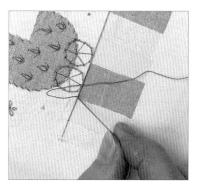

16. Use single chain stitch to work up two pale and two deep pink flowers as shown on the template, then finish the background with a few French knots in pale and deep pink.

17. Use a single strand of blue cotton thread to make a long stitch across the top of the patchwork pavement.

18. Go back along the line couching the thread down with tiny stitches. Bring the thread up and down through the same hole.

19. Work straight stitches down the vertical lines and couch these down as before.

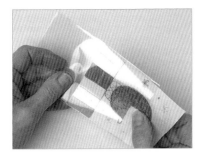

20. Spray with water to remove the marker pen lines, press and trim the fabric to size, then slide it into the polypropylene bag.

21. Place the bag on the front of the card and make a small pencil mark at the top centre.

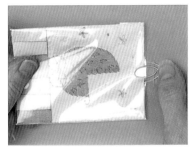

22. Open out the card, use a craft knife to cut a small slot for the decorative paper clip, then fit the bag with the enclosed embroidery on the front of the card.

Tip
Shaped paper clips can make a decorative addition to a card. You can buy them in your local craft shop or make your own from fine enamelled wire.

The finished card

Appliqué is a quick method of applying large areas of colour to an embroidery design and allows you to keep your stitching to a minimum. Because of this it is ideal for celebration cards or handmade invitations for the main guests at a wedding.

Using card blanks with a luxurious finish such as these translucent or frosted finish cards will enhance the colours of the beautiful silk dupion.

The polypropylene bags used for these cards are sold by card companies. Scrapbook suppliers normally have a wide range of decorative paper clips, eyelets and snaps that can be used to attach your embroidered designs to the card blanks.

Bouquet of flowers
Stitching with ribbons

Ribbon embroidery uses many ordinary embroidery stitches such as French knots and split stitch. The most popular designs are floral because the flowers look so attractive in ribbon. You can just make up the flowers and leaves as you go along or learn to use stitches such as ribbon stitch for leaves and loop stitch to make the stunning dog rose for a more realistic effect.

You will need

Two-fold, oval-aperture, raspberry card, 11 x 15.5cm (4¼ x 6⅛in)

4mm wide silk ribbons: yellow, raspberry, green and fuchsia

4mm organza ribbon: blue

White fabric

Cotton backing fabric

Embroidery hoop

Embroidery scissors

No. 18 chenille needle

No. 9 crewel needle

Six-stranded embroidery cotton: lime green, yellow and pale blue

Water-soluble marker and water sprayer

Iron

Low-loft wadding

Double-sided sticky tape (DSST)

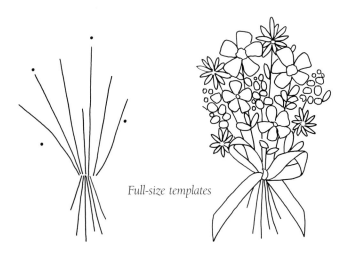

Full-size templates

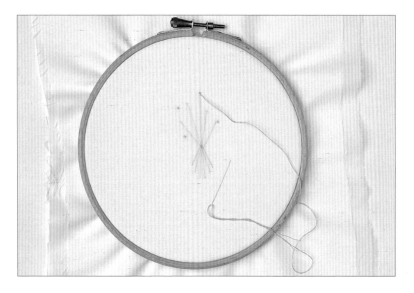

1. Use the water-soluble marker to direct trace the stems on to the white fabric. Mark dots for the centres of the yellow daisies. Layer with the white cotton backing fabric and fit into the embroidery hoop. Thread two strands of lime green thread on the crewel needle and anchor them on the back of the fabric adjacent to the top of the longest stem. Start the split-stitch stem by bringing the thread up through the top of the stem.

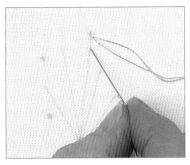

2. Take needle down through the fabric approximately 6mm (¹/₄in) along the stem . . .

3. . . . bring the needle back out half way along the previous stitch and pass it between the two strands of cotton.

4. Continue by pulling the thread through and taking the needle down through the fabric 3mm (¹/₈in) down the stem. Repeat for the other stems as marked.

5. Thread a 25cm (10in) length of yellow ribbon on to the chenille needle. Bring the ribbon out at the centre of a daisy, leaving about 6mm (¹/₄in) of the ribbon on the reverse side to anchor it.

6. Work a straight stitch out from the centre to the tip of a petal, then bring the needle back up through the centre of the daisy.

7. Repeat step 6 to work a series of petals for each daisy. Trim the end of the ribbon to 6mm (¹/₄in).

8. Using raspberry ribbon, bring the needle out at the centre of a rose, leaving a 6mm (¹/₄in) tail on the underside. Take the needle back through the same hole . . .

9. . . . then, using the eye end of a needle to control the ribbon, gently pull the ribbon through to make a loop.

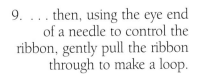

10. Repeat steps 8–9 to make four more loops. Make three more roses in a similar way.

11. Use two strands of yellow cotton to work a straight stitch down each petal and a French knot at the end of each straight stitch.

12. Work a two-loop French knot with yellow ribbon in the centre of each rose.

13. Use the blue organza ribbon to make a series of French knots for the delphiniums. Use two strands of pale blue thread to make the smaller florets at the top of each flower head.

14. Work ribbon stitch for the leaves. Start by bringing a length of green ribbon out at the stem. Lay the ribbon flat and take the needle through the ribbon where the end of the stitch will be . . .

15. . . . then gently pull the ribbon through from the back until its end curls over to form the leaf shape.

16. Repeat steps 14–15 to make groups of ribbon-stitch leaves on each rose stem.

17. Still working with the green ribbon, make straight-stitch leaves for the stems of the daisies and delphiniums.

18. Lay the card on top of the embroidery, then use the water-soluble marker to make a series of dots 5mm (^{3}/₁₆in) in from the oval aperture.

19. Bring a length of blue organza ribbon out on the marked oval, lay it along the oval and, using three strands of blue cotton, couch it down every 6mm (¹/₄in).

20. Tie a bow with a length of fuchsia ribbon and stitch in position on the bouquet.

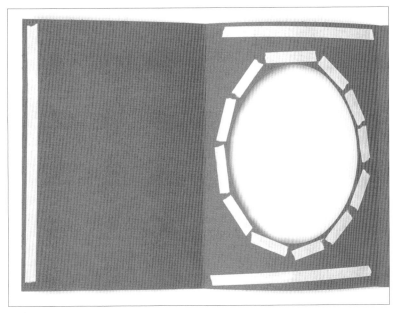

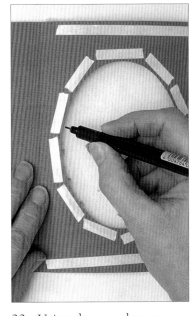

21. Apply short lengths of DSST around the aperture and long lengths across the top and bottom and down the edge of the inside flap.

22. Using the template as a guide, mark and cut out an oval of wadding.

23. Spray the embroidery with water to remove the marker lines, press to remove creases, then, referring to page 27, mount the embroidery in the card.

Tip
You can stitch flowers in any colour of ribbon you like. Why not buy ribbons in a themed pack to create a subtle coordinated bouquet?

The finished card

Ribbon embroidery is ideal for stitching flowers and it is just delightful watching the designs come to life as you 'arrange' the flowers one at a time. Floral designs are particularly effective arranged realistically in bouquets or wreaths or even in a wicker basket. To make the basket simply sew lines of sheer ribbon across the basket area and then weave silk and sheer ribbon through the horizontal ribbons to create a woven effect.

Cuddly Cat

Stitching in long and short stitch

Long and short stitch is a simple stitch used to cover areas of fabric in solid stitches. It is easy to shade areas of the design by working subsequent rows in a slightly lighter or darker colour of thread. This design also uses satin stitch to work the horizontal bands across the cat's body and to fill in its eyes. To prevent the design puckering as you stitch, bind the inner ring of the embroidery hoop with narrow white tape before you begin so that the fabric can be stretched tightly.

You will need
Two-fold, oval-aperture, turquoise card, 15 x 20cm (6 x 8in)
White fabric
Backing fabric and an embroidery hoop
Water-soluble marker and water sprayer
Six-stranded embroidery cotton: white, pale, medium and dark grey/brown, black and bright blue
No. 9 crewel needle
Embroidery scissors
Low-loft wadding
Dressmaker's pins
Double-sided sticky tape (DSST)

Full-size template

1. Referring to page 36, trace the design on the white fabric, then layer with the backing fabric in the hoop. Thread two strands of the medium grey/brown cotton and bring the thread up through the fabric at the top of the head, just to one side of an ear.

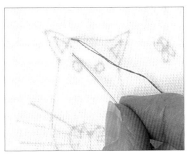

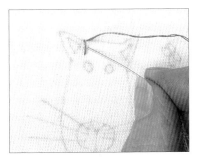

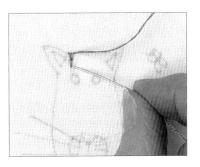

2. Make a long vertical stitch by taking the needle down through the fabric 6mm (¹/₄in) below the start point . . .

3. . . . bring the thread up beside the previous stitch, then make a short stitch, say 3mm (¹/₈in) long.

4. Now work another long stitch beside the short one.

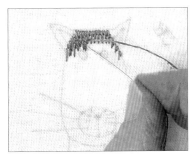

5. Continue the series of alternate long and short stitches across the head and down in front of the ears.

6. In the next row, bring the needle up through the previous stitches, and make the new stitches more random in length.

7. Continue working down the face area, leaving spaces for the eyes and nose and create a random edge at the bottom for the shading.

9. Change to the dark grey/ brown thread and work a row of long and short stitches below the face for the start of the neck. Change back to the medium grey/brown, work another row of stitches to fill in to the top of the black band. Use the same thread to work the first row of the body below the black band.

8. Change to the pale grey/ brown thread and add the shading. Bring the needle out through the previous stitches, make a series of long and short stitches that follow the curved bottom edge of the face.

Tip
Keep the long and short stitches close together so that none of the background fabric shows through.

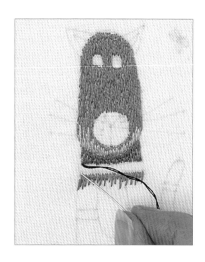

10. Fill in the band on the neck with satin stitch. Using two strands of black cotton, bring the needle up at the top left-hand corner and back down at the bottom corner.

11. Pull the thread through, bring the needle up at the top, just to the side of the first stitch, and back down at the bottom. Work across the band, keeping the stitches close together.

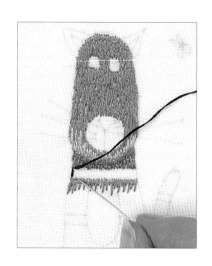

12. Fill in the rest of the body with long and short stitch.

Work the main part of the body with medium grey/brown thread.

Use pale grey/brown and white threads to create the breast panel.

Use medium and pale grey/brown to shape the legs, then add white on the paws.

Use white, all three shades of grey/brown and black to embroider the tail.

Use pale grey/brown and white to fill in the nose.

Work the outer parts of the ears with pale grey/brown then fill in with white.

Fill in the other bands on the body, legs and tail in satin stitch with black thread, then add some highlights with medium grey/brown thread.

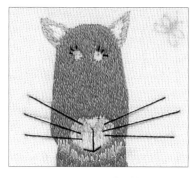

13. Use one strand of black cotton to work straight stitches for the whiskers, mouth . . .

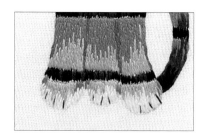

14. . . . and the claws.

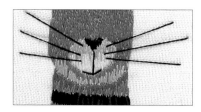

15. Fill in the nose with black satin stitch.

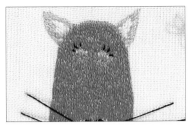

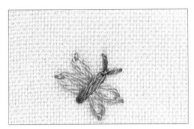

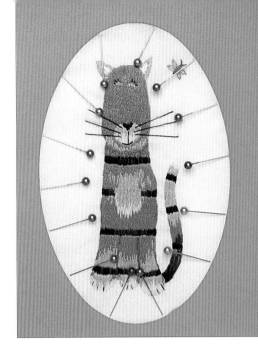

16. Fill in the eyes with blue satin stitch. Using one strand of cotton, work a small white straight stitch at each corner of the eyes as highlights and small black straight stitches for the eyelashes.

17. Use two strands of blue cotton to work four single chain stitches for the wings of the butterfly. Use two strands of dark grey/brown to work one long single chain stitch for the body and two short straight stitches for the antennae.

18. Remove the embroidery from the hoop, lightly spray with water to remove the marker pen lines, then press to remove creases. Place the aperture of the card on top, use dressmaker's pins to mark the shape of the aperture, then cut the wadding to size. Finally, referring to page 27, fit the stitched piece and the wadding into the card.

Tip
Choose a card that matches the colour of the embroidery thread used for the eyes and the butterfly.

The finished card

Many people associate long and short stitch with natural subjects such as flowers and birds as you can create such realistic designs with subtle shading. These fun animals are in keeping with the natural subject but are much less complicated to stitch. Use the stitched designs as a guide to create a template or draw your own fun animals to stitch.

Index

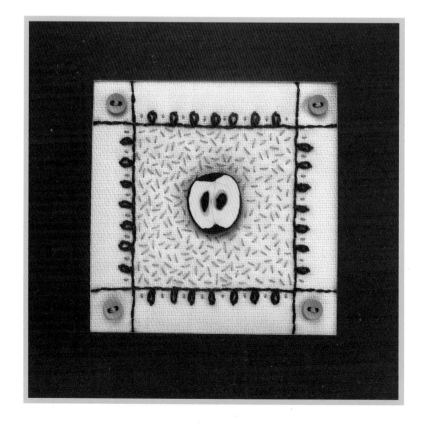